Lonely Planet

50 Beaches

TO BLOW YOUR MIND

Contents

Parties // Social & nightlife beaches

Encounters // Wildlife & conservation hotspots

Family // Calm, safe all-rounders for all comers

Introduction

Let's face it; the beach that will next blow your mind is more than likely the next one you can get to, regardless of where it is.

We love beaches, despite their many inconveniences. The impolite, pushy and un-shy sand. The temperamental surf. The wind that whips hair, sand and surf into a frenzy. The sun that burns that spot the sun block cream didn't reach. The sharks that stalk us (thankfully, usually, in our minds alone).

Yes, we love them. A beach always feels like the ultimate escape. Why? Is it an evolutionary hangover? Are we returning to our ancient origins as creatures-crawled-out-of-the-ocean? Or did we develop our desire for the beach alongside our need for the food that the ocean provides? Is it the sound of the waves, which science says has a calming effect on our brain activity? Maybe it's the guaranteed hit of vitamin D our exposed skin absorbs.

We could speculate all day. Except that brings us no closer to the beach. And at the beach, there'll be no speculation; we'll be in the moment. So go! Find a beach. Go now. Don't wonder why. You know it's the right thing to do.

Bliss // Tropical desert island paradises

Cabbage Beach / Nassau, Bahamas

THE NAME OF THIS BEACH ISN'T CONJURING UP AN IMAGE OF PARADISE.

Ignore the somewhat ignoble name and focus on the impossibly white and soft sand, the nearly 3km of aquamarine waves gently lapping at the shoreline, the tropical tiki huts providing shade along the length of the seashore, and the palms swaying in the warm breeze.

WELL IT SOUNDS LIKE IT'S A TEXTBOOK EXAMPLE OF PARADISE.

There's no denying the Bahamas know how to do beaches. The only off-putting thing about a holiday here is that everyone else wants to holiday here. Cabbage Beach is very, very popular – so expect to share your sunshine.

CAN I AVOID THE CROWDS?

There are a few options. You can see the land from the sea by renting a jet ski or a more sedate floating lounge from one of the multitude of operators. You could retreat to one of the luxury resorts that ring the coastline and order yourself a cocktail. Or tune out the masses with a pair of giant sunglasses and your own beachside sun lounger. If all this fails to get you the solitude you crave, try heading to the eastern end of the beach where it's slightly less populated.

IAN CUMMING © GETTY IMAGES

Crane Beach / Barbados

WILL I SEE A CRANE? THEY'RE SO BEAUTIFUL.
Um, I think you might have the wrong crane in mind. The winching kind gave its name to this beach, though thankfully it's no longer a feature. It wouldn't really suit the scene: this destination is another beach that rarely misses out at the 'best beaches in the world' awards. In place of the crane you do have the Crane, a 100-plus-year-old hotel resort that sits elegantly high up on the cliff with a glass elevator that takes its guests down to the perfect pink-hued sands and the blissful blue water below.

I JUST WANT TO JUMP INTO THAT WATER!
Go crazy. With the fair waves that keep rolling in, it's a great beach for boogie boarding and body surfing.

I BELONG THERE, I THINK.
You and everyone else. But there are other ways to enjoy the beach. To blaze your own trail, follow the road to the beach another 500m east and you'll come to a cow pasture where a path leads you to a long, quiet strip of sand. Picnic? Check. Sunbathing? Check. Best day of your life? Got to be a chance.

Flamenco Beach / Culebra, Puerto Rico

I FEEL LIKE DANCING ACROSS THE SAND.
With a mile of sheltered beachline, you can dance all you like. And you'll be doing it in style: Playa Flamenco is generally regarded as the finest in Puerto Rico. Best in the Caribbean even, according to some. Either way, people don't talk that way for no reason.

I'M NOT GOING TO ARGUE.
If you go on a weekday, you're sure to come away with a sense of its beauty. Weekends can get very busy, but it's well serviced and even the crowds are unlikely to dim your view. You can camp here too – see the stars reflected in the clear, mirror-like bay. If the mood takes you, have a piña colada at one of the kiosks. Doesn't that feel right?

SURE. BUT WHY IS THERE A TANK AT THE END OF THE BEACH?
Don't worry, it's not loaded! It is a remnant from the days of war games practised here, but now it's a work of art. Or unconventional camouflage, to say the least!

Green Island Beach / Green Island, Antigua & Barbuda

THIS IS JUST WHAT A DESERT ISLAND LOOKS LIKE IN MY MIND.

The place is practically deserted, with turquoise water as far as the eye can see and lush greenery flanking the white sand. Green Island Beach comes straight out of tropical island central casting.

IT'S HARD TO BELIEVE WE'LL GET THIS SLICE OF PARADISE ALL TO OURSELVES.

Of the Antiguan islands, Green Island is your best bet for some privacy: it's out of the way and can only be reached by charter boat. Once you're on the island there are a number of secluded beaches to explore with Green Island Beach being on the even-more out-of-the-way west coast.

WHAT'S ON THE ITINERARY?

It's a packed schedule of sunbathing, snoozing and snorkelling. Not necessarily in that order.

GOOD SNORKELLING TO BE HAD?

Calm and clear, the water stays relatively shallow for a way out to sea so it's perfect for gently bobbing around with your head immersed. The rock formations around the edges of the cove make for some interesting exploring too.

Hanalei Bay Beach / Hawaii, USA

IT'S A PRETTY NAME FOR A BEACH.
Pretty name for a stupendously pretty place. Often cited as Hawaii's most beautiful beach (which is kind of gobsmacking considering the competition!), Hanalei has all the trappings: calm, sheltered waters, mountains as the backdrop, boats moored in the bay, white sand and, yep, you guessed it, clear clean water.

IT LOOKS KIND OF FAMILIAR.
Seen one beach seen 'em all? I don't think so. But maybe you recognise it from its starring role alongside George Clooney in *The Descendants* or, if you're a little older, in *South Pacific*.

A street back from the beach and you can have a drink (or a meal) at Tahiti Nui – the tiki bar is perfectly Hawaii. You might recognise it as well...

MOVIE-STAR BEACH!
Natural talent shines through. You can play an active supporting role though. Try your hand at sailing, snorkelling, windsurfing and swimming of course.

AND AFTER ALL THAT?
At the end of the day you can add a sunset walk along the pristine sand. Relaxing, romantic, scene-setting.

Nalaguraidhoo Beach / South Ari Atoll, The Maldives

YOU COULDN'T SWING A COCONUT AROUND THE MALDIVES WITHOUT HITTING ONE OF THE WORLD'S BEST BEACHES.

It's true, there isn't a 'best beaches' list worth its salt that doesn't include one from around here, so picking the best of the bunch is a really tough exercise. If the jaw-droppingly gorgeous, cyan-hued seas of Nalaguraidhoo don't float your boat then jump aboard an inter-island water ferry and find your own slice of paradise.

TELL ME MORE ABOUT THE BEAUTIFUL NALAGURAIDHOO.

If a picture tells a thousand words then the photo of Nalaguraidhoo just keeps saying 'paradise' over and over. You could lie forever staring at the azure waters surrounding your private thatched villa or get up close to the sea life snorkelling or diving around the reefs. There's a full-service spa if this activity gets too strenuous.

IT'S NOT SOUNDING LIKE THE CHEAPEST HOLIDAY I'VE EVER HAD.

There's no getting around the fact that a luxury locale like this comes with a hefty price tag. The Maldives is not a place renowned for being a budget-traveller mecca; it might be that you'll have to save your pennies for a visit to this once-in-a-lifetime experience.

Orient Beach / St Martin

I WAS EXPECTING THE CARIBBEAN IN A LIST LIKE THIS...SO WHY THIS BEACH IN PARTICULAR?

There are miles of Caribbean coastline hosting more white sand and crystalline waters than you can throw a sunbed at. The Orient Beach doesn't disappoint on this picture-postcard front. However, here there is more, or should we say less...?

NOW WHAT'S THAT SUPPOSED TO MEAN?

At the Orient less is more. Or so say that majority of sun lovers who mostly choose to enjoy the spectacular surrounds without their swimsuits on.

AH I SEE, IT'S ONE FOR THE NATURISTS THEN.

Not only. Although the Club Orient Resort at the beach's southern end is the island's only nudist resort, the beach itself is 'clothing optional', so you can keep your swimmers on if you don't feel like letting it all hang out.

MAYBE A DRINK WOULD HELP ME LOOSEN UP...

You're in luck. There are bars and restaurants lining the sand, so sit back and enjoy the, ahem, view. Or, if you're feeling restless, get into some of the beachy activities like jet skiing, paragliding and sailing.

Shoal Bay / Antigua

DID YOU PHOTOSHOP THAT PICTURE?
Maybe a tiny bit, you know, just to make it look like it does in real life. Because IT REALLY DOES look like this.

BRING ME A SUN LOUNGER, NOW!
It's all you need. This beach really is out of the pages of a luxury escape magazine. The sand is so fine and white it's like walking on confectioner's sugar. And there are 3km of it! The sweet life continues with water that takes the picture-in-the-dictionary spot next to 'crystal clear'. Combine this perfection with bars and open-air restaurants, deck chairs and loungers... you know what to do.

IF I DO DRAG MYSELF INTO ACTION, WHAT DO YOU RECOMMEND?
The off-shore coral reef means spectacular snorkelling or diving (and you can see it in a glass-bottomed boat as well). If that all sounds a bit much, then just amble down to the gently rolling water to give yourself a healthy sparkle before heading back to the chore of lying down in the sun.

Source d'Argent Beach / La Digue, Seychelles

DO I DETECT A FAINT HUE OF PINK IN THAT SAND?

Crazy right? As if a beach like this needed any enhancement, the addition of the pink sand really ups the ante in the picture-postcard stakes.

SO I'M TICKING OFF ALL THE BOXES ON MY TROPICAL PARADISE CHECKLIST.

It really is the stuff of fantasy. You've got a secluded cove combined with swaying palm trees and calm crystalline aquamarine waters, oh, and that unforgettable pink-hued sand. There are huge, weathered granite boulders that bookend the shoreline, which makes for a dramatic backdrop in your real-life image of paradise.

IT'S UNLIKELY I'LL WANT TO MOVE FROM THE BEACH, BUT IF I GET BORED...?

Bored? Are you having me on? Lie back and listen to the water lapping at your toes. Take a deep breath of the fragrant air. Saunter up to one of the nearby restaurants to sample some of the Creole-inspired cuisine. If all this fails, you can charter a helicopter to see if the sand is any pinker on any of the other 115 islands in the Seychelles archipelago. That should spice things up a bit.

Trunk Bay /
St John, US Virgin Islands

ANOTHER CARIBBEAN WONDERLAND?

Feeling a little spoiled by all this beach perfection, are we? Yes, Trunk Bay is a wonderland. In fact, it's a beach that is consistently in top-10-beaches-of-the-world lists – no matter who makes them.

SO IT'S CROWDED THEN?

You won't be alone, there's no denying it. Not even a day-use fee for the beach turns people away. The beach has lifeguards, is well serviced with nearby restaurants, bars and accommodation and is kind of spectacular – and that will be just your first impressions.

THERE'S MORE?

Strap on a mask and snorkel (you can hire them there) and hit the snorkelling trail, which guides you through a snowdome-effect of fish and coral. Gin-clear, as divers say. The surface is the turquoise of your dreams and there's fine coral sand leading away from the beach to hiking trails. But stay awhile, splash around – it's too good to be true.

Drama // Wild & unusual beaches

Bowling Ball Beach / Mendocino, California, USA

BOWLING BALLS?

This striking (thank you, thank you very much) beach is part of the Schooner Gulch State Beach reserve. It's one for the beachcombers, photographers and geologists, no question. The spherical rocks (specifically, 'concretions' – packed sandstone eroded into the balls you see) almost look like a strange family from a Disney film, rolling in to greet you.

THESE ARE SOME FREAKY BOULDERS.

Rock hopping is a lot of fun (take care, they can be slippery), but go at low tide to get the full experience. Find a little rock pool and explore a microcosm of sea life. You'll probably be alone, as this is not a high traffic beach: the whales passing by off-shore will be all yours to enjoy.

WHAT'S THE WATER LIKE?

Feel like a little surfing? You can do that here. Windsurfing too. The swimming is good and there are hiking opportunities as well. You want a perfect day for the family? Well then, just pack a picnic and your swimming costumes, explore the balls, collect some salty souvenirs from the caves and crags, and take a dip.

Giant's Causeway / County Antrim, Northern Ireland

I'M NOT GOING TO NEED A BUCKET AND SPADE FOR THIS ONE, AM I?

No, this is not your typical beach experience. Declared a World Heritage Site by Unesco in 1986, these ancient, interlocking volcanic columns rise dramatically out of the North Atlantic Ocean and spread for miles along the base of the basalt cliffs in County Antrim.

CAN I FOLLOW IN THE GIANT'S FOOTSTEPS AND WALK OVER THE COLUMNS?

Yes, it's possible to clamber over the 60-million-year-old lava formations make-believing you're tracing the path of the legendary giant, Finn McCool. As part of your adventure keep an eye out for the even odder shaped rocks like the Giant's Boot, or the Camel Hump.

AND WHAT ARE THOSE HUGE FINGERS OF STONE I CAN SEE REACHING FOR THE SKY IN THE DISTANCE?

They're known as the Chimney Stacks. Surrounding columns have eroded over time and left these free-standing stacks looking like chimneys, or some say like cathedral spires. The illusion of a man-made structure is so convincing that in 1588 the Spanish galleon, *La Girona*, opened fire thinking it was Castle Dunluce, before foundering on the rocky coast, killing nearly everyone on board.

Gulpiyuri Beach / near Llanes, Spain

WOW, THIS IS SOMETHING YOU DON'T SEE EVERY DAY.

This beach is a definite contender for Most Extraordinary. A flooded sinkhole with its own 40m-long sandy beach backed by steep granite cliffs set like an ocean jewel in a green meadow just 100m from the Cantabrian Sea. We are not making this up.

NO WAY! HOW IS IT THAT I CAN SEE LITTLE WAVES IN THE WATER?

This is because the Cantabrian Sea has slowly eroded away the land, forming a series of underground tunnels joining Playa de Gulpiyuri with the waters of the Bay of Biscay and making the beach totally tidal. It's not exactly surfs-up, but it's a fun phenomenon to splash around in.

I BET THIS GETS COMPLETELY OVERRUN WITH FANS.

On the weekends there's an influx of international tourists and you'll certainly have to jostle for space on the sand. Weekdays, however, are much quieter; you may even be lucky enough to get a touch of that private-island vibe.

Hidden Beach / Puerta Vallarta, Marieta Islands, Mexico

AN UNDERGROUND BEACH? SOUNDS LIKE THE STUFF OF LEGEND.

Just look at this place. Have you ever seen a beach so remarkable, so other-worldly, so enticing?

HOW IS THIS EVEN POSSIBLE?

The uninhabited Marieta Islands exist as a result of ancient volcanic activity, though it's rumoured that the spectacular formation that is the Hidden Beach was caused by explosives of the man-made kind. The islands were used as a military testing ground by the Mexican government in the early 1900s – could this magnificent structure be the result of a secret bomb?

IT'S JUST SET A BOMB OFF IN ME!

There's no need to worry. In 1995 the islands were declared a national park and were henceforth hosts to purely peaceful human activity.

HOW AM I EXPECTED TO CLIMB INSIDE?

There is no way of entering the Hidden Beach from the surface. The only way in is through a long tunnel, hewn from the rock, that runs from the Pacific Ocean under the lush green surface to the beach. Swimming or kayaking is your only means of transport. Stifle any claustrophobia and make the journey as it's well worth it – you'll see what we mean once you get there.

Hot Water Beach / Coromandel Peninsula, New Zealand

ARE WE HOT TUBBING?

DIY style. When you visit this beach, a spade is a required piece of kit. Two subterranean fissures allow hot spring water to bubble up through the sand. Grab your spade and dig yourself (and your friends) a cosy little Jacuzzi and let the warmth surround you.

SERIOUSLY? HOW HOT ARE WE TALKING?

The water reaches around 60°C which, when mixed with a little sand and sea water, is pretty much perfect. The springs bubble into life a couple of hours either side of low tide so make sure you check your tide charts before making the trek to the Coromandel Peninsula. It can get busy: try visiting the Hot Water Beach on a rainy day for some peace (you're only going to get wet anyway!)

GOTCHA.

That said, this beach is not just about the soft-sand hot tub. There's surf if you go that way, there's art galleries for some indoor highbrow action, and cafes to make your day of pampering complete.

DAY SPA!

Your very own. Just take care out there – the ocean could give you an unexpected full-body massage with waves breaking over your tub.

Punalu'u Beach / Hawaii, USA

HAWAII!

Yep, just spells beach doesn't it? But here's a different one for you. Black sand! In a way, it's iconic of Hawaii – it comes from lava cooling into basalt as it hits the ocean and breaking up. Because 'Hawaii', of course, also spells volcano...

WHAT DOES BLACK SAND FEEL LIKE?

It's kind of coarse and pebbly – this is not the super-fine sand of your Tahitian paradises. It's precious too – to a point. The point being that you're not allowed to take sand from this rare kind of beach with you (except for what presumably gets stuck in the usual places), so no collecting in jars.

IT JUST SEEMS KIND OF WEIRD.

It is odd. Punalu'u is in many ways the quintessential Hawaiian beach: palm-fringed, rolling blue surf – it's just that the bit in the middle is at the complete opposite end of the light spectrum. Go with the flow.

NICE ONE. WHAT SHOULD I PLAN TO DO THERE?

It's a photographer's dream, strange scenery that it is. It's a great beach for walking and exploring – and seeing the hawksbill and green turtles, two endangered species that call the beach home. As for swimming, it can be a little risky with strong rips and...yes, you need to be wary of sharks.

Vik Beach / Vik, Iceland

ICELAND? BEACH? ARE YOU CRAZY?

Calm yourself and take a look. See. You don't have to swim to get pleasure. This place takes the striking black-sand beach vibe to another level with its pretty awesome rock formations – the hexagonal basalt steps and of course, the Icelandic trolls in the waves.

TROLLS?

Um, we meant basalt sea stacks – mini mountains rising from the sea. But legend has it they are the remains of trolls that were petrified as they attempted to drag ships out of the sea.

IT ALL SOUNDS KIND OF FAIRY-TALE.

With a reputation for being the wettest place on the planet, the gloom, the black sands, the craggy trolls, the basalt columns leading up the face of the cliff...yes, it does have a fantasy tinge to it. Throw in caves as well (where a dangerous monster is said to have once dwelled) and it's getting positively epic. Did we mention it's at the base of an active volcano?

I'M ALL CREEPED OUT.

On the less scary side, there's a large puffin community. Weird looking, but not dangerous...

Action // Surfing & diving meccas

Bells Beach / Victoria, Australia

THIS PLACE IS THE STUFF OF SURFING LEGEND.
Even if you're too young to remember the last scene from
Patrick Swayze's 1991 surfing classic, *Point Break*, it's enough
to let you know that the film closes on Bells Beach – 'cause it's
the place where you'll catch some of the world's most
epic waves, dude.

GNARLY, RIGHT?
Like, totally. Bells is situated along a stretch of coastline in
southern Australia known as the Great Ocean Road. The
shoreline along the road is world famous and hosts some of
the most dramatic coastal scenery in the world. Steep cliffs rise
sharply out of the reef-scattered shallows, and it's these reefs
themselves that create the excellent breaks needed for those
surfing waves.

OK, LET'S HIT THE WAVES.
Easy, tiger. Despite its popularity and renown, Bells Beach is
not a place for beginner boarders. The regularly large swell
that rolls in from the Southern Ocean hits exposed reefs
and creates a sharp break and testing conditions, even for
experienced surfers. If you're keen to see how the experts carve
it up then make your way down over the Easter break when the
beach hosts a pro surfing competition.

Biarritz Beach / Biarritz, France

TIME TO GET OUR GLITZ ON.

The name 'Biarritz' does conjure up images of bejewelled 19th-century nobility 'taking the waters' and strolling along the promenade against a backdrop of art nouveau palaces. It is true that Napoleon III's wife, Empress Eugenie, had a palace built next to the water in 1854 which would served as her summer villa.

AM I IN THE RIGHT PLACE?

Though the palace still stands and functions as the luxury Hotel de Palais, in more recent years, the beach resort has grown a reputation for stellar sets of waves over royal beach goers.

THERE GOES THE NEIGHBOURHOOD THEN.

The upmarket hotels and popular turn-of-the-century casino still keep the well-heeled travellers coming and there's no denying the celebrity allure of the place – star-spotting is on the activities agenda for sure.

BEACH BUMS AND MOVIE STARS?

The beach garners a fun and eclectic mix of travellers and locals, which creates a party-like atmosphere and a thriving tourist scene. So you can expect to rub shoulders with all sorts of folk, as well as share time in the waves with an international cast of surfers.

Bondi Beach / Sydney, Australia

AS AUSSIE AS A MEAT PIE.

A trip to Sydney wouldn't be complete without jostling for space on the sand with every other man and his dog on the shores of Bondi. The beach is an iconic tourist spot and a beloved local hang-out so expect a mixed bunch of cheerful sun worshippers.

THERE'S A WHOLE SWAG OF BEACHES IN SYDNEY. WHY BONDI?

Bondi has everything. Clear Pacific Ocean surf rolling in on creamy white sand; lush, green parkland directly back from the water, perfect for picnics or a game of football; and a strip of world-class shops, restaurants and bars that keeps the beach pumping past sundown.

WHAT IF I'M LOOKING FOR A LITTLE LESS PARTY AND A LITTLE MORE PEACE AND QUIET?

Take a stroll along the 6km coastal walk from Bondi to Coogee and stop off at one of the quieter coves like Bronte or Tamarama. During the summer months the walk hosts an annual outdoor sculpture exhibition by local artists called 'Sculpture by the Sea'.

50

Ehukai Beach / Hawaii, USA

WHOA, LOOKS LIKE I NEED TO GET THE BOARD OUT FOR THIS ONE.

You may not have heard of Ehukai but if you've got any love for the sport of surfing then the words Banzai Pipeline will set your pulse racing.

DO I GET YEAR-ROUND BARREL ACTION?

It's the winter months that bring the best of the swells to Oahu's north shore. These swells push up on a shallow reef creating pipeline waves that are the stuff of dreams for surfers the world over.

CAN BEGINNERS GET IN ON THE ACTION?

The Banzai is generally best left to the professionals or at the very least the super-experienced. If you're not overly confident in your board-riding skills then take a seat on the edge of the water and watch the experts carve it up.

SURFING SCHMURFING, WHAT ELSE IS NEWS?

In summer the swell around Oahu dies right down and the sea opens itself up to some fantastic snorkelling. Then, when you're done swimming for the day, head to nearby Sunset Beach to experience the island's best view of the setting sun.

Popoyo Beach / Tola, Nicaragua

WE'VE HEARD THAT THIS BEACH HAS SOMETHING TO DO WITH A PINK PANTHER. THAT'S WEIRD.

This remote and tricky-to-get-to surf beach is signposted for keen-eyed travellers with a meditating pink panther positioned on the side of the road. Alight from your overcrowded chicken bus at the pink panther and continue on foot down a dirt road towards the glistening salt plains.

PINK PANTHERS, SALT PLAINS, CHICKEN BUSES – QUITE A MAGICAL MYSTERY TOUR.

Oh, one more thing. You'll also need to heft your bags up on your head and then wade through the Salinas de Nahualapa River to reach the tiny town of Popoyo before you even make your way to the beach.

THIS BETTER BE WORTH THE EFFORT.

We haven't seen a disappointed surfer yet.

SO IT'S ALL ABOUT THE SWELL?

There's not really any other reason to be here. The little town has just one convenience store, a couple of hotels, a few restaurants and a popular surf hostel which hums with the excited ranting of blissed out wave-riders. Rent a board from the hostel and get in the water. You'll be guaranteed steady decent-sized sets that you can pretty much call your own.

Tallow Beach / Byron Bay, Australia

CAN THESE PLACES PLEASE BE A LITTLE CLOSER TOGETHER?!

With almost 36,000km of coastline, you're going to have to travel to get to some of Australia's most spectacular beaches. Byron Bay on New South Wales' northern coast is worth the trip though.

WHAT'S SO SPECIAL ABOUT IT?

Apart from the fact that the beaches are beautiful, the vibe is laid waaaaay back (this place has a strong hippy history) and food and drink is close at hand – particularly at Tallow, which is in the heart of the town.

I AM WELL UP FOR LAID-BACK.

Don't let the world pass you by, though. How many town beaches give you whale watching alongside the usual suspects of surfing, swimming and sunning? It's also a good fishing beach, so bring your tackle.

DUDE, CHILL OUT A LITTLE.

Ah...ok. Well, you've found a little enlightenment then. It's not surprising. So just relax on the beach till evening comes and the lighthouse sends out its beams to keep you enthralled. Then mosey into town when a snack seems the right idea. You'll be very happy here.

Wayag Beach / Raja Ampat, West Papua, Indonesia

I THINK I MAY HAVE DIED AND GONE TO DIVING HEAVEN.

If you love life under the sea, then this is where you will want to be. Pulau Wayag is one of the many small islands in the Raja Ampat archipelago. The stunning atolls and striking karst (limestone) formations make for fabulous snorkelling and deep sea diving with the rocks supporting an enormous amount of sea life.

I COULD EXPLORE THIS UNDERWATER DISPLAY ALL DAY LONG.

If the epic diversity of the underwater display somehow becomes too much, or perhaps your skin starts to sprout scales, it's a lovely idea to walk to the highest point on the island where you can take in a breathtaking bird's-eye view of all the mountains, coves and secluded sandy beaches.

AFTER A DAY OF DIVING AND CLIMBING I'M READY FOR A COOL BEER BACK AT THE HOTEL.

Dream on. This is a remote archipelago with very few facilities and that's part of its charm. Most visitors to Wayag choose to base themselves on a live-aboard – a small cruise boat that provides food and board and drops anchor wherever you want to explore next.

Discovery // Beaches for combing & exploring

Charmouth Beach / Dorset, UK

I WANT TO MAKE A CRACK ABOUT THE UK AND BEACHES.

I'm sure it would have been funny. In any case, the only cracks you need to make here are in the rocks you kick around on the beach – this is fossil paradise. The side of the beach west of the river mouth is the best spot – but remember, keep your fossicking to the stones and rocks on the foreshore – no digging into the cliff face. If you can't find yourself a prehistoric relic, then you're not trying hard enough. In fact, you're not trying at all!

I DON'T WANT TO TRY TOO HARD AT THE BEACH.

Fair enough. Then defy the global expectations of English beaches and hit the sand and surf. Yes, surf too! The beach to the east of the river has more sand (fewer rocks and fossils) and is very family friendly. There's a beach cafe off the beach for your ice creams and a nice picnic area with tables as well.

I TAKE BACK THE CRACK.

See, it's not all grey and cold. Except for the fossils. They are definitely grey and cold.

Conche des Baleines / Île de Ré, France

I CAN SEE A LIGHTHOUSE BEAMING IN THE DISTANCE.

You can climb Le Phare des Baleines lighthouse for magnificent, sweeping views of the remote and expansive Île de Ré coastline. Here's a suggestion: while you're up there, pick out a spot in the grassy dunes to spread out your picnic blanket.

OH, SO I CAN BUY LUNCH FROM SHOPS ALONG THE SHORELINE?

Mais non – nothing so commercial and crass; you're in France. Instead you can go and explore one of the quaint little Gallic villages that bookend the beach for typically French local produce like cheeses, terrine, pate, fresh bread, etc, to pepper your picnic rug.

I GET THE FEELING IT'S A BEACH FOR ALL SEASONS.

Combing the coast for seashells on the Conche des Baleines is as beautiful in winter as it is in summer. There are bikes for hire in the nearby villages which can see you winding along quiet cycle paths through the beautiful pine groves on the edges of the sand, and most importantly, the legendary sunsets are a spectacular sight all year round.

Navagio Beach (Shipwreck Beach) / Zakynthos, Greece

OMG.

Completely. It's 87 kinds of beautiful coming at you all at once. Secluded, protected by vertical cliffs that tower above, sparkling azure as imagined by Greek gods, pure, perfect sand and, just to give it an extra bit of character, like a beauty spot on a face, a shipwreck!

I JUST WANT TO GO THERE NOW. CAN I PLEASE GO THERE NOW?

Easy as can be – as long as you're in Zakynthos. If you are, there are a number of towns, Porto Vromi for example, from where you can take a boat to paradise. It is as you see it – there are no amenities – so you'll need to bring with you all the supplies you need for the time you're on the sand/in the water/ exploring the shipwreck.

HOW DID THAT WRECK GET...WRECKED?

It was a smuggler's ship caught doing its dirty work in 1982. During bad weather a while after the seizure, the boat was washed up on the shore where it was left to rust.

IT JUST LOOKS SO AMAZING!

To get a view of the beach from on high, visit the village of Anafonitria. There's a platform at a monastery there and the sight of the bay below you will make you wish you were there. And then, of course, you can be!

Squeaky Beach / Wilson's Promontory, Australia

I HAVE TO ASK: WHY SQUEAKY?

Fine round grains of sand ensure your feet will sing their way from one end of this miraculous beach to the other.

IT COULD GET A LITTLE GRATING.

First-world problem.

POINT TAKEN.

You need to unwind. As we're in a national park, try a hike. While you can drive in to a beach access point (leaving you with a 5-minute stroll to the sand), there are a number of amazing walking trails to get to know the surrounding Australian bush before hitting the surprisingly turquoise waves. (A small warning: the water is almost always on the icy side.) Despite its relatively easy access, you'll not be wanting for space – it's a quiet beach, even in summer, thanks to its national park location. That means it's a bring-your-own-everything experience.

SO QUIET TIME IS THE ORDER OF THE DAY?

If you're looking for a little activity, the north end of the beach has a maze of granite boulders which will keep you entertained. But yes, apart from the squeakiness, you can expect plenty of quiet and calm.

Strathy Bay / Sutherland, Scotland

WE APPEAR TO BE IN THE WILDS OF THE SCOTTISH HIGHLANDS.

Not every awesome beach experience is of the tropical variety. The remote, sandy cove of Strathy is on the northern coast of the Scottish mainland, staring out to the cold expanse of the North Sea – the setting is ruggedly beautiful. The beach is wide and perfect for a romantic evening stroll along the sand.

I CAN'T SWIM AND I'M DONE WITH WINDSWEPT WANDERING, WHAT NOW?

If you're feeling adventurous there are some caves and interesting rocky stacks to clamber around at either headland.

CAN I GET TO THAT LIGHTHOUSE OVER TO THE WEST?

Yes, you can. If you start out at the car park at Strathy Point you can walk up to the Strathy Point Lighthouse. Up here is a perfect vantage point to take in the sweeping views of the ocean as well as the surrounding crofting landscape.

ALL THIS HIKING ABOUT IN THE CRISP SCOTTISH AIR IS MAKING ME THIRSTY.

Well you don't have to venture too far to quench your thirst. Lucky for you the nearby Strathy Inn is happy to pour you a wee dram.

Tierra del Mar / Oregon, USA

THE 'BEAVER STATE' HAS A BEST BEACH IN THE WORLD?

It does indeed. Oregon being one of only three states in the contiguous US to have a Pacific Ocean coastline (this doesn't include Hawaii or Alaska) you can find yourself in an exceptional brooding atmosphere along this wild and open 3km stretch of sand.

SO I CAN'T EXPECT SUN LOUNGERS AND COCKTAILS ON THIS ONE?

This beach has more your moody, windswept vibe of long, introspective walks in serene and spectacular scenery.

SOUNDS A BIT SERIOUS.

Then saddle up for some adventure. There are riding stables that take you out to the beach on horseback and allow you to gallop through the shallows. That should get your heart racing.

WHOA NELLY!

Come back down to earth with some sedate beachcombing. Tierra del Mar is famous for washing up beautiful agates and the collectable Japanese glass floats – hollow glass balls once used by fishermen to keep their fishing lines afloat. While the floats are no longer in use there are many still drifting in the Pacific Ocean and can be found washed ashore.

Tra Ban (White Strand) / Renvyle Peninsula, Ireland

NOW THIS IS AN INSPIRING SIGHT.
And you're not the first person to think so. Renvyle House, which sits on the Renvyle Peninsula, was once home to William Blake and his family and was a favourite retreat of WB Yeats and Oscar Wilde.

THERE MUST BE SOMETHING SPECIAL ABOUT THIS PART OF THE WORLD.
Picture the vast white shoreline being met by the clear aquamarine waters that come rolling in from the Atlantic Ocean, and the hinterland is a classic scene of bucolic beauty. It's poetry in motion.

WHAT'S THE BEST WAY TO EXPERIENCE THE BEACH?
Believe it or not, the brave can strap on their scuba gear and get under the water, though if you'd rather admire the ocean from more of a distance there are horse-riding tours along the coastline. It's also a popular place for a spot of fishing. Locals will let you know the better cast-off points.

IT'S EASY TO SEE HOW THE WHITE STRAND EARNED ITS WORLDWIDE REPUTATION.
Be sure to stick around and watch the sun set behind the crumbling ruins of 13th-century Renvyle Castle.

Parties // Social & nightlife beaches

Bačvice Beach / Split, Croatia

THIS LITTLE COVE LOOKS LIKE IT'S SMACK BANG IN THE CENTRE OF TOWN.

There are stunning beaches running the length of the Dalmatian Coast but it's always nice to find an urban one that shares the same clear Adriatic water as its stunning cousins further south. And it's one that you can simply roll onto from your city launch pad.

PROMISE IT'S NOT GOING TO BE OVER-POPULATED AND POLLUTED?

We can't promise much on the crowd situation (hey, people-watching here is part of the attraction!) but the water is clear and cool and a welcome respite from the hustle and bustle of the city.

WHAT'S GOING ON WITH THE WEIRD GAME OF VOLLEYBALL EVERYONE IS PLAYING?

That would be *picigin*, a sport that is native to Split. It works a little bit like volleyball, but without the net. You can play it in the water by sorting your fellow game-players into two opposing teams and the aim of the game is to prevent the ball from landing in the sea.

I'M EXHAUSTED JUST WATCHING EVERYONE AROUND ME PLAY.

You can revive and refuel by heading a few metres back from the beach to the three-storey pavilion where you can choose between a number of cafes and bars from which to see in the night (and beyond).

Copacabana / Rio de Janeiro, Brazil

A NAME I KNOW.
It may not be the most beautiful beach in the world but it is certainly one of the most famous.

TOP 5 MAYBE.
That's what happens when a hit song features your name.

THAT SONG WASN'T ABOUT THE BEACH.
People only hear the chorus. And it was conceived in Rio, so, you know, close enough. Anyway, the beach...

YES, LET'S TALK ABOUT THE BEACH...
This 4km stretch of action-packed beachy goodness has become party central in Rio. One and a half million people watched the Rolling Stones perform here!

WHAT ELSE IS IN STORE?
The beach zones off into interest areas: west of Copacabana Palace is the gay and transvestite section, known as the Stock Market – look for the rainbow flag. Footballers hold court near Rua Santa Clara while next to Forte de Copacabana is the unofficial *posto de pescadores* (fishermen's post).

IT SOUNDS BUSY!
Copacabana is a beach with a city of millions just a few metres away. And it won't let you forget that for a minute.

Gulf Shore Beach / Alabama, USA

ALABAMA HAS REALLY BEEN KEEPING QUIET ABOUT THIS ONE, HASN'T IT?

You can't blame the locals for trying to keep this coastal gem to themselves, but unfortunately (or fortunately, for the rest of us) the word is out and there are a growing number of devotees of Alabama's glorious white-sand beaches.

TELL ME MORE ABOUT THESE SOUTHERN-STYLE BEACHES.

Gulf Shore and its sister seaside attraction Orange Beach are the popular points along a 50km stretch of squeaky clean sand. These days the whiteness is peppered with multicoloured beach umbrellas shading families, couples, teenagers, tourists, locals...basically anybody who loves being by the seaside. If you feel like a crowd, visit during the Hangout Music Festival – top acts perform and you can lose yourself amongst 35,000 other fans before hitting the waves.

WHAT ABOUT WHEN THE CURTAIN IS PULLED?

Paddle-boarding, jet skiing, beach volleyball, big game fishing, and dolphin-watching tours are just a few of the activities on offer. Our personal favourite though is the zip line at the Gulf Adventure Center: from 27m off the ground you get the best view possible of the sprawling coastline.

50

Paradise Beach / Mykonos, Greece

PARTY TIME!

Yes, it's time to let it all hang out, this is your party zone. It's a young crowd (and we mean CROWD!) and hedonism is the order of the day. And the night. You can expect to start early and in all likelihood not stop until it's time to leave. And on Paradise Beach there's no need to bring a book. Reading's for old people.

OUCH. COOL, REFRESHING WATERS MAYBE?

Take a dip. Take a drink with you. Don't stop dancing. To be sure, the water is beautiful, rich golden sand fringes the waterline and the sky is blue. But the place is just not so much about the sand and surf. It's about the pumping beats and the quest to make a connection with your fellow partiers. It's about stamina and making this the best night of your life. Over and over again.

I'M GOING TO FIT RIGHT IN.

That's the spirit! You'll find more hostels than you can poke a stick at, and the resorts veer towards nightclubs, so in both cases sleeping is not the priority. Who'd want to sleep in paradise anyway?

South Beach / Miami, Florida, USA

THIS LOOKS LIKE SHINY MIAMI AT ITS SUN-KISSED FINEST.

Be prepared for a supercharged seaside experience in South Beach. Here everything is bigger, brighter and louder. The area is as world-famous for its nightlife as for the daylight action on the beach.

BOTTOMS UP, IT'S PARTY TIME.

South Beach pumps day and night with tourists and locals cruising the coastline. There's something for everyone. You can jump in with a group of like-minded souls for a game of volleyball at the water's edge or simply lie back and people watch to your heart's content. When the sun sets the countless bars and clubs come into their own – join the throng of beautiful people all queuing up to get in to the most popular of venues.

I'M PARTIED OUT, WHAT IS THERE TO DO IF MY LIVER NEEDS A BREAK?

South Beach has some great shopping and there are countless designer shops and boutiques to help you part with your money. If keeping the hip pocket happy is part of the plan just have a meander around the streets back from the shoreline and check out all the stunning art deco architecture.

Venice Beach / LA, USA

I'M PICTURING ROLLERBLADES AND BODYBUILDERS.

It's exactly what you imagine it to be, based on the countless images of it that have been broadcast around the world over the decades. It's the quintessential urban beach with one of the most varied displays of human life you can see – aliens might consider this a good place to start explorations.

DO PEOPLE ACTUALLY SWIM THERE?

Well, you have to make it past the visual smorgasbord-walk first. There are the basketball courts where you can see some out-of-this-world skills on display. There are the street vendors and performers who work their magic. There's Muscle Beach Venice where iron is fully pumped. And then, seriously, you have a great beach, for swimming, surfing – choose your pleasure. The beach is wide and the lifeguards have their eyes out for you.

IT ACTUALLY SOUNDS KIND OF EXHAUSTING.

You could be right – this is the ultimate beach for those who can't just switch off for more than an hour – the entertainment (whether in nearby bars and other venues) endless activities in store and people watching means boredom is practically impossible on Venice Beach.

White Beach / Boracay, Philippines

THIS IS STARTING TO HURT.

In a crowded field for title of most ridiculously perfect beach, White Beach makes a bold statement of intent. You want to be here? Of course you do.

TOOK THE WORDS RIGHT OUT OF MY MOUTH.

What makes it so stunning is that you will not be alone and it's quite commercial and developed, yet you'll feel like it's all yours. And you can do almost anything you want here. White Beach is the centre of the action, its 6km of super-soft sand and aqua waters are home to water sports of every flavour. Diving is almost a must: if you haven't done scuba before, this would be an ideal place to get wet.

I'M FEELING A SPECIAL CONNECTION TO THIS PLACE.

Well maybe a full-moon beach party is on the cards then: you can get in touch with your spiritual side at one of these monthly parties. And even if you're not the party type, there's a good chance that watching the sun set on this west-facing beach might also be a transcendental moment. It's worth a shot anyway.

Encounters // Wildlife & conservation hotspots

Agonda Beach / Goa, India

FUNNY, I NEVER THINK OF INDIA WHEN IT COMES TO BEACHES.

Well it is probably better known for its river (you know, the Ganges) but the south of India and Goa in particular can take you to paradise pretty quickly. Agonda Beach is a great example.

WHY'S THAT?

It's perfect really. Actually, it's not the perfect swimming beach; the high tide conceals steep drop-offs and the surf gets a bit unruly. But don't take that the wrong way: you can certainly still wade in and have a swim!

SHARKS?

Not that we're aware of, but watch out for the olive ridley turtles – there's a nesting site and a protection centre that looks after this vulnerable species.

SO WHAT IS IT PERFECT FOR?

Romantic walks along its simple beauty – it's a wide, open beach and really is very pretty. At sunset, it has that extra special something. It's relatively quiet and isolated, though not far from more touristy action if you need some of that. It's got that really cool, relaxed vibe to it, without it being in the middle of nowhere.

Diani Beach / Mombasa, Kenya

WILL I SEE MONKEYS?

Funny you should say that – yes, you will. Diani might just
be the beach that caters to every person's beach needs.
Wildlife, 10km of sand, beach resorts as well as more modest
accommodation, water sports, camel rides...

CAMEL RIDES?!

Don't knock it till you try it. It's not the wildlife we spoke
of, but how often do you get to ride a camel on a beach?
As for wildlife, there are your monkeys at nearby Colobus
Conservation and if you can tear yourself away from their
antics, take a day trip to Shimba Hills National Park where you
can see elephants, leopards, antelope and more monkeys.

WHAT ABOUT THE BEACH?

It's got fine white sand, clean clear water, a rainforest at the
fringes (often disguising resorts) – it's a beauty. And there's
virtually nothing you can't do here. Once you jump off your
camel, there's skiing, kitesurfing, snorkelling, fishing... and
swimming of course.

APRÈS BEACH?

This is a well-serviced beach: you can find numerous
restaurants, shops, a shopping centre and bars. We're not
talking big-city stuff here, but there's more than enough to add
an extra dimension to your beach escape, though it's highly
unlikely you'll get bored with all that's in store.

Espiguette Beach / Le Grau du Roi, Languedoc Coast, France

THIS COULD BE THE END OF THE EARTH.
Part of its appeal is that Espiguette is wild and free, backed by miles of sand dunes, lagoons and salty scrubland. Aside from the 27m-high lighthouse in the distance there isn't a man-made structure to be seen.

SOUNDS WILDLY ROMANTIC.
The further you walk from the car park, the more 'romantic' the beach gets. That's code for nude, in case you were wondering.

SO I SHOULDN'T BRING GRANDMA FOR A PICNIC?
A fair distance to the west of the car park is the area well-known as a naturist and gay hangout. So perhaps steer Granny in the other direction. The beach is so large though that you'll have no trouble finding a private patch of sand to call your own for the day. There's every chance that your nearest neighbour will be a gorgeous pink flamingo.

UM, EXCUSE ME? DID YOU SAY FLAMINGO?
We did! The shallow lagoons behind the beach attract spectacular wild pink flamingos, who like to congregate in the Camargue. The Camargue is the only place in France and one of the only spots in the Mediterranean where they can be seen.

Manuel Antonio Beach / Puntarenas, Costa Rica

COSTA RICA EQUALS ADVENTURE. RIGHT?

And then some. Here you are in Manuel Antonio National Park. There are mountains and forests and more wildlife than you could possibly imagine. You can hike till you drop, and when you drop, make sure you do it at this beach.

ARE YOU GETTING SICK OF ALWAYS USING THE WORD 'PARADISE'?

You'll notice I didn't actually say that. But it's the price you pay for a job like this. It's called hyperbole-fatigue. But luckily there's a beach to fix that ailment. Let's say it's this one.

WHAT SHAPE DOES THE CURE TAKE?

I'm going to start with a little monkey-spotting – there are four kinds that call the park home. Then I'm going to exit the forest to the beach, I'm going to lay out a towel, pull out a sandwich and a drink from my bag (there are bars in town, but you need only enter the park to find wilder shores) and empty my mind of words as I enjoy the simple pleasure of just being on the beach and keeping it all to myself.

I WON'T DISTURB YOU.

Shhh...

Maruata Beach / Michoacan, Mexico

YOU CERTAINLY GET YOUR MONEY'S WORTH HERE.
Three for the price of one. Along the gorgeous expanse of smooth yellow sand there are three distinct sections of the Maruata Beach that will satisfy every part of one's beach-going desires.

OK, LAY IT OUT FOR ME.
Snorkellers and those who just want to float around in pristine, clear waters please make your way to the eastern, crescent-shaped end of the beach. This is where the freshest seafood can be bought and you're also allowed pitch a tent. The more adventurous of you will enjoy a vigorous swim in the middle section before climbing the headland and exploring the many caves and tunnels. At the far right or western end of the beach is where you'll find the wildest of the surf and also a hard-to-reach, secluded cove where the weighty shackles of swimwear can be discarded.

DIDN'T I HEAR SOMETHING ABOUT TURTLES ON THIS BEACH?
Amid the humans who enjoy the array of natural wonders along this popular coastline there are many black sea turtles who like to build their nests and hatch their eggs every night from late June to December.

Matira Beach / Bora Bora, French Polynesia

CAN THIS BE REAL?

We're going to give it to you straight: when all's said and done, **there can be only one beach, one beach to rule them all. This** is it. It's phenomenal. Sublime. It's Bora Bora. It's the South Pacific of your dreams.

BORA BORA OR MATIRA BEACH?

Bora Bora has about 25km of beaches, but a great number of them are private – you'll find that you need to stay in the resort that has pinned itself to the shore (in some cases, pinned itself to the water!) in order to enjoy their beaches. But Matira Beach, here, is open to the public, basically the only one in Bora Bora that is. And. It. Is. Stupendous.

FREE IS GOOD.

Free and spectacular is even better. It just gets better and better. As if the sheer postcard-paradise-blue of the water wasn't enough, you don some snorkelling gear and get smacked with the clearest water and seriously friendly fish. Really colourful fish, and turtles and dolphins and all manner of ocean life. Richness above and below the waves. (When we say 'waves' we mean 'gently lapping perfection'.)

Monkey Mia / WA, Australia

THIS IS THE DOLPHIN BEACH, RIGHT?

Yes – confusingly, not a monkey in sight. The delightfully friendly bottle-nosed dolphins have been drawing a crowd to this Western Australian beach for more than 50 years now. No small feat, considering where Monkey Mia happens to be located – around 900km north of the WA capital city of Perth – which is pretty much in the middle of nowhere, in case you were wondering.

900KM? NOT A DAY TRIP THEN?

Getting there is an adventure in itself. There are four flights per week from Perth to the Shark Bay resort at the edge of the beach, or you could take a leisurely two-day drive up the coast. That gives you some perspective on how gigantic the island nation of Australia really is.

WILL THE DOLPHINS BE HAPPY TO SEE ME IF I COME ALL THIS WAY?

You can trust them! These adorable cetaceans can be relied upon to turn up every day and will swim right into the crystal-clear shallows in order to be fed. The rangers from the Department of Parks and Wildlife are there to vigilantly supervise the human/dolphin interaction to ensure the dolphins' safety.

Family // Calm, safe
all-rounders for all comers

Brandinchi Cove / Sardinia, Italy

I WAS EXPECTING STUNNING MEDITERRANEAN-STYLE BEACHES, BUT THIS LOOKS NEXT LEVEL!

This is known as 'Little Tahiti' in Sardinia, and throughout the rest of Italy, because of its shallow, cyan-coloured waters and fine white sand. It's true: Cala Brandinchi is more reminiscent of the South Pacific than an Italian island.

OH, SO MUCH FOR MY MEDITERRANEAN HOLIDAY, THEN. BUT I CAN WORK WITH THIS!

You won't be alone. The 700m of pristine sand is very popular with locals (and tourists), especially families with little ones in tow, because of the calm, shallow water.

AFTER THE SANDCASTLE WORK, WHAT DO YOU RECOMMEND?

Snorkelling is a very popular pastime considering the quiet sea, but if you're looking to get your heart rate beyond floating speed it's possible to rent paddle boats and kayaks to cruise around the beautiful bay. If you really want to leave the crowds behind there are motorboats for rent which means you can explore further afield around some of the nearby hidden coves.

Koh Kood (Koh Kut) / Trat Province, Thailand

WHY ARE WE HOPPING ALL THE WAY OVER TO THIS LITTLE ISLAND?

It's true that there's no shortage of choice when it comes to beautiful beaches and stunning tropical islands in Thailand, but it is rare to find one that retains some of that elusive undiscovered vibe.

SO NO BOATLOADS OF TRAVELLERS FLOCKING TO FULL MOON PARTIES HERE?

You won't have the island to yourself but we can guarantee you won't be sharing it with 700 backpacking mates. This is a more family-friendly place with little night life to speak of.

WHAT IS THERE TO SEE AND DO ON THIS SLEEPY-SOUNDING ISLAND?

On the west coast of the island you will find the best of the island's beaches. They're often bordered by undeveloped plots of land and have a remote and private feel. This means that you have a chance of getting the whole place to yourself. If you feel the need to break up the tedious routine of lying around on a private beach on a tropical island then consider a hike to one of the spectacular waterfalls and swimming holes. Klong Chao is the largest of all the falls and sometimes has tour groups visiting in the afternoons. Klong Yai Ki is smaller and quieter.

Porthcurno / Cornwall, UK

THIS LOOKS LIKE QUITE THE SUNTRAP.
Indeed. Seeing a gorgeous little bay like Porthcurno makes you think that the Brits may just be keeping schtum to the rest of the world to get their stunning beaches all to themselves.

THIS BEACH LOOKS LIKE IT COULD BE IN THE RIVIERA OR OFF THE CROATIAN COAST.
Doesn't it just? Instead, it's a little cove just 4km from Land's End, the most westerly point of the English mainland.

SO CAN I ASSUME IT'S A HIDDEN GEM?
Not exactly. While the world goes about thinking all British beaches are windswept and rugged, the people of Cornwall and surrounds are happily sunning themselves in their slice of coastal paradise. The beach is popular with families: kids love to play in the freshwater stream that runs down into the surf.

THAT'S A PRETTY IMPRESSIVE ROCK FORMATION AROUND THE COVE.
The 65-tonne rock you can see balancing on the Treen Castle cliffs is known as Logan's Rock. It used to sway back and forth in fierce winds but after it was pushed into the sea by some unruly soldiers in 1824 it was raised back to its resting place and secured to prevent it from being dislodged.

Praia de Mira / Mira, Portugal

YOU DON'T HEAR MUCH ABOUT PORTUGAL'S BEACHES.

Shhh, let's keep it that way. Locals know all about this beautiful location but it's not on the tourist trail, so it has a laid-back, family-friendly atmosphere.

LET ME IN ON THE SECRET.

The long, soft-sand beach is 300m wide and is dotted with brightly-coloured fishing boats and painted wooden huts. In fact, you'll know you've found the right place when you spot the striped wooden fisherman's chapel perched at the edge of the beach. The whole place is picturesque and unpretentious.

UNPRETENTIOUS? YOU MEAN SIMPLE?

Not at all. Part of the appeal of the area is the mix of coastline and the quiet lagoon which gives you plenty to do. It's perfect for paddle-boating, sailing, canoeing, windsurfing and swimming. The pine forest around the lagoon has several trails and is a charming spot for an afternoon stroll. You can also hire a bike and cycle the flat paths.

I'M GOING TO NEED SUSTENANCE AT THIS RATE.

Then it's fortunate that there are several cafes lining the beach. They can supply you with fresh seafood that comes in right off the water is a speciality and goes perfectly with a *cerveja* as the sun starts to set.

Will Rogers State Beach / Malibu, California, USA

THIS SOUNDS GLAMOROUS ALREADY.

It may be named after a silent movie star, but that's just the start of it. You are about to dip your toes into a genuine star of film and TV. Recognise it? The lifeguard towers. The red one-piece bathing costumes on the female lifeguards. The hairy chest of the red-shorted boss lifeguard. Are you feeling it...?

NO! *BAYWATCH*?! GET OUT!

Il nothing else, I expect there to be a few shots of you taken running along the beach in slow motion. (For the record, *Baywatch* eventually moved to Hawaii for filming, but this is where it all began.)

IT LOOKS LIKE A VERY PLEASANT BEACH.

You know what, it really is. It's beautiful and long, the swimming is great, it's not crowded, there are plenty of facilities, you can learn to surf, play volleyball, kayak, kitesurf...you can even fish! And it's popular without being overcrowded (unlike Santa Monica Beach up the road), giving it a bright friendly vibe. Pleasant indeed.

AND THE HOFF?

Your human *Baywatch* star is unlikely to make an appearance, but Will Rogers quietly makes up for the absence. You won't miss a beat.

About the authors

Ben Handicott once published travel pictorial and reference books, dreams about, writes about and sometimes even does, travel. Growing up inland, he loves the beach but sees sharks in every wave.

Kalya Ryan is a travel writer, editor and has been a beach-junkie since her first sand castle on Sydney's beautiful Bronte Beach. A sentimental favourite, Bronte now has competition for personal top spot since her discovery of Mexico's stunning Hidden Beach.

Index

Africa

Asia

Europe

North America

Cabbage Beach, Nassau, Bahamas 12

Crane Beach, Barbados 14

Ehukai Beach, Hawaii, USA 56

Flamenco Beach, Culebra, Puerto Rico 16

Green Island Beach, Green Island, Antigua & Barbuda 18

Gulf Shore Beach, Alabama, USA 86

Hanalei Bay Beach, Hawaii, USA 20

Hidden Beach, Puerta Vallarta,
Marieta Islands, Mexico 40

Manuel Antonio Beach, Puntarenas, Costa Rica 104

Maruata Beach, Michoacan, Mexico 106

Orient Beach, St Martin 24

Popoyo Beach, Iola, Nicaragua 58

Punalu'u Beach, Hawaii, USA 44

Shoal Bay, Antigua 26

South Beach, Miami, Florida, USA 90

Tierra del Mar, Oregon, USA 76

Trunk Bay, St John, Virgin Islands 30

Venice Beach, LA, USA 92

Will Rogers State Beach, Malibu, California, USA 122

Oceania

Bells Beach, Victoria, Australia 50

Bondi Beach, Sydney, Australia 54

Hot Water Beach, Coromandel Peninsula,
New Zealand 42

Matira Beach, Bora Bora, French Polynesia 108

Monkey Mia, WA, Australia 110

Squeaky Beach, Wilson's Promontory, Australia 72

Tallow Beach, Byron Bay, Australia 60

South America

Copacabana, Rio de Janeiro, Brazil 84

Published in May 2016 by Lonely Planet
Publications Pty Ltd
ABN 36 005 607 983
www.lonelyplanet.com
ISBN 978 1 76034 059 9
© Lonely Planet 2016
Printed in China
10 9 8 7 6 5 4 3 2 1

Written by Ben Handicott and Kalya Ryan

Managing Director, Publishing Piers Pickard
Associate Publisher Robin Barton
Commissioning Editor Jessica Cole
Art Direction Daniel Di Paolo
Layout Designer Hayley Warnham
Editor Bridget Blair
Picture Researcher Christina Webb
Print Production Larissa Frost, Nigel Longuet
Cover image Justin Foulkes

Lonely Planet offices

AUSTRALIA
Level 2 & 3, 551 Swanston Street,
Carlton 3053, Victoria, Australia
Phone 03 8379 8000
Email talk2us@lonelyplanet.com.au

USA
150 Linden St, Oakland, CA 94607

Phone 510 250 6400
Email info@lonelyplanet.com

UNITED KINGDOM
240 Blackfriars Road, London SE1 8NW
Phone 020 3771 5100
Email go@lonelyplanet.co.uk